Advance Praise

"If you are willing to do what few others are willing to do for a period of five years in your twenties, you can live the rest of your life like few others can! In Jeff Johnson's new book, *One Decade to Make Millions*, Jeff has masterfully detailed the HOW and the WHY!

Jeff's educational, experienced, and real-life stories leave each reader off at the intersection of 'Desire' and 'Willing To Do' with the tools to make it happen.

Simply read this classic and decide to act now!"

—JIM LUNNEY, CFP, FOUNDER OF THE WEALTH STRATEGIES GROUP, DENVER, COLORADO

"Having spent several decades working in the financial services industry, I have observed, time and again, the benefits related to disciplined saving and investing early in life. *One Decade to Make Millions* provides information and real-life stories that will resonate with readers while driving home this important concept. I won't hesitate to share this book with my two twenty-something daughters."

—CYNTHIA H CHENEY, RETIRED COMPLIANCE DIRECTOR AND HEAD OF REGULATORY SUPERVISION AT A TOP-10 WEALTH MANAGEMENT FIRM

"Author Jeff Johnson was my personal finance instructor at the University of Nebraska. Using his teaching, my wife and I have become financially successful at a young age. *One Decade to Make Millions* includes all of Jeff's core teachings that everyone should learn. I hope what you learn in this book will change your life as it changed ours!"

—VICTOR ANDRADE, OPERATIONS MANAGER AND INVESTOR

"Getting started early in life makes the likelihood of financial success much greater. *One Decade to Make Millions* is a book that explains why it's important, as well as the first important steps a young person should take."

—LARRY SWEDROE, AUTHOR OF *YOUR COMPLETE GUIDE TO A SUCCESSFUL AND SECURE RETIREMENT*

"Most young people are unprepared to take the steps now to begin laying the foundation to have a healthy financial situation in the future. One Decade to Make Millions teaches the intentional decisions young people can make to attain the financial future they want and need in a very accessible format."

—GEOFFREY BROWN, CAE, CHIEF EXECUTIVE OFFICER OF THE NATIONAL ASSOCIATION OF PERSONAL FINANCIAL ADVISORS

"As a financial professional for over forty years, I have seen the dramatically different results from starting your savings and investing in your twenties versus a decade later. One Decade to Make Millions is the book that shows the way. Every young person should get or be given a copy of this book."

—GERRY FINNEGAN, CFP, REGISTERED INVESTMENT ADVISOR AND LECTURER IN FINANCE AT THE UNIVERSITY OF NEBRASKA—LINCOLN

"I took a financial course taught by Jeff Johnson in college that I feel should be required for every student, regardless of their major. I followed Jeff's guidance and, ten years later, have confidently built a solid financial foundation for myself and my family. *One Decade to Make Millions* is a college semester of lessons and stories condensed into one readable book. Every young person should have a copy to help set themselves up for success upon entering their professional career."

—BRADEN ZYSSET, STRATEGIC BUSINESS DEVELOPMENT MANAGER AT NEBRASKA MEDICINE

"*One Decade to Make Millions* shines light on the critical topic of financial literacy to start building wealth at a young age and teaches these life lessons through an easy-to-read book and narrative storytelling. Working in the financial world my entire career, I can tell you investing early in life can make all the difference. This book is a must read for generations to come and a great gift to someone starting off in their financial life journey."

—WENDY HARTMAN, CFP, PRESIDENT AT BUCKINGHAM STRATEGIC WEALTH

One Decade to Make Millions

One
Decade
to Make
Millions

A STRATEGY TO MAXIMIZE

THE POWER OF YOUR TWENTIES

Jeff C. Johnson

LIONCREST
PUBLISHING

ONE DECADE TO MAKE MILLIONS
A Strategy to Maximize the Power of Your Twenties

FIRST EDITION

ISBN 978-1-5445-3092-5 Hardcover
      978-1-5445-3091-8 Paperback
      978-1-5445-3090-1 Ebook
      978-1-5445-3093-2 Audiobook

For Kaiya and her generation.

Contents

Introduction

The Bookkeeper got a practical education and earned fair but modest pay. The Surgeon was highly respected and made more than $1 million annually for many years. Of the two, who had the most money saved when it came time to retire? One has lived a stress-free life, financially confident—and retired with money to spare. The other needed a retirement Plan B at the end of his working career.

Which one do you choose to be?

If you are a recent or soon-to-be graduate from high school or college, I wrote this book for you. The perfect time to learn financial skills is when you are just starting to earn an income from employment. This is the best time in your life to start putting intentional money habits to work in your life right away. This book is not intended to be a detailed deep dive into the financial world. It's about getting started building a foundation for future financial wellness now, when time is on your side.

However, if you prefer to live large right now, you're likely thinking you can save for your child's education, a dream home, or retirement later in life. This mindset is not uncommon today in America. Hey, if that's your choice, you can go straight to the back of the book where I'll help you start your Plan B thinking. But… you might want to read from the beginning, keeping in mind that saving in your twenties has the greatest impact on your life savings. Go ahead. Turn the page to begin Chapter 1: The Bookkeeper's Story and the Surgeon's Story.

The stories in this book are true, with names and some details altered to respect the privacy and confidentiality of personal information. Illustrations and examples are provided for general information and educational purposes. There are instances throughout the book where the author may present a hypothetical case study regarding client returns or growth of a portfolio over time. These cases are for illustrative purposes only, rely on several underlying and implied assumptions, and should not be considered as a demonstration of actual performance results. Past performance is no guarantee of future results.

Chapter 1

The Bookkeeper's Story and the Surgeon's Story

WHICH LIFESTYLE IS RIGHT FOR YOU?

For nearly forty years as a wealth advisor, I've observed my investment advisory clients' financial choices—and perhaps have learned more from them than they've learned from me. Some taught me what works when it comes to financial success. And from others, I've learned what does *not* pan out so well.

The Bookkeeper's story and the Surgeon's story are examples of contrasting lives and lifestyles.

The Bookkeeper and I met in the early 1980s when

I made an in-person visit to his office. I was a young stockbroker, out looking for clients. I asked him to open an investment account with my firm, which he eventually did.

After high school, he graduated from a two-year business school and started working in the accounting department for a local company. He and his wife were raising three young children in a nice middle-class home and drove late-model used cars. The Bookkeeper's initial transaction with my firm was $2,000, which was placed in a very conservative investment.

Over the years, the Bookkeeper added to his portfolio. He rarely withdrew money and was never forced to sell investments, because he always had a cash reserve fund set aside for emergencies and large purchases. This cash reserve allowed him to buy, for example, cars or major appliances whenever necessary and avoid borrowing money. Therefore, he had few monthly payments. This left extra money after paying household bills, allowing him to save and invest regularly over the years.

ON THE WAY TO WEALTH

When a relative left the Bookkeeper an inheritance, he added the $50,000 sum to his investment account. He always pointed to investing—rather than spending—this windfall as the event that really got his financial portfolio rolling.

The Bookkeeper's family benefited from a secure and tranquil home, shared social activities, and college education funds for the children. As his income grew and his family obligations were reduced, he was able to accelerate his spending and his saving. Since he and his wife did not have elaborate material desires, they spent some and also increased their savings rate.

Almost forty years later, the Bookkeeper and his wife are living in the same comfortable home and have few financial concerns. They've never purchased a brand-new car, opting instead to be more financially savvy by purchasing pre-owned vehicles and saving thousands—perhaps millions!—of dollars.

Their now-adult children are established and living well. They are saving money and building their own financial worlds, following the lifestyle they learned while growing up.

The Bookkeeper might have lived humbly, but his financial finesse left him with the option of retiring in his early sixties—with an investment account worth more than $5 million, far more than he will need to live comfortably in his lifetime. He always earned a modest salary, and his wife never worked outside the home. Because of their solid financial footing, she was able to be a full-time mom and homemaker, but was also free to volunteer for important community projects and causes.

Throughout their lives they have given generously to charities, usually anonymously. They make practical gifts to their children and help fund college savings plans for their grandchildren. They travel, work in their garden, and spend a lot of time with friends and family.

In my mind, they are very wealthy in every way.

DOCTORING AND DOWNSIZING

The Surgeon was well known in our community and highly respected in the medical field. He and his wife were the parents of adult children who had been educated at the best private universities. They lived in a large custom home in a prestigious neighborhood.

They drove brand-new luxury cars and enjoyed a high-profile social image. The couple appeared to enjoy a very high standard of living, as they were members of country clubs and were involved with many prominent organizations in the community.

Shortly before his retirement, the Surgeon hired me to help plan his retirement income. I was pleased and eager to work with him, anticipating he could become a substantial client of my firm. But when I reviewed his finances, I discovered a problem. After earning millions in his professional career, he had accumulated only enough money to provide for five or six years of retirement income at the level he had identified as a livable amount.

Additionally, there were significant credit card debts and a second mortgage on his home. The cash in his savings account was barely enough to make the following month's payments. After a high-earning professional career, the Surgeon's net worth was far less than the Bookkeeper's net worth.

I recommended a dramatic change in lifestyle—what I call a Plan B. It involved a significant reduction in spendable income for the rest of his life. This also meant the sale of the five-bedroom house and right-sizing to a smaller home. Their Plan B also included a switch from three leased luxury cars to more affordable alternatives, as well as the elimination of several expensive activities and memberships. It also cut out hope for elaborate travel plans and required a delay in the Surgeon's retirement.

Somehow, my suggestions took the couple by surprise. Then that surprise turned to disbelief and, eventually, disappointment. When the recommended lifestyle changes were implemented, the Surgeon and his wife were embarrassed about the publicly visible shift in their circumstances.

This account of the Bookkeeper and the Surgeon is true, with details altered to protect the privacy of the individuals. I know many people with financial traits similar to the Bookkeeper's as well as many others who share the same plight as the Surgeon.

The Bookkeeper's lifestyle and financial choices provide the pattern for the steps I recommend in the following chapters. On the flip side is the Surgeon, an example of someone who did not find the discipline to apply common-sense rules for handling his finances and instead expected that his high income might somehow stretch into eternity.

It's probably easy to imagine the Bookkeeper, given his background in finances, as thrifty and intuitive in developing a plan for saving and investing. The truth is that people who have traits like the Bookkeeper in this story come from all walks of life and every level of income.

However, it's a common misconception to look at high-income people living expensive lifestyles and incorrectly assume they are wealthy. Sadly, many not only have financial problems ahead but also often end up suffering from other issues that are likely stress-related.

You see, I've learned that people who have financial well-being almost always benefit in nonfinancial ways. They experience less work stress and worry in life, and tend to have happy marriages and family situations. They enjoy a calm feeling about money that is the result of having a sense of financial confidence and security.

But not everyone wants to live the lifestyle of the Bookkeeper in this story. Some people still elect to take the path of the Surgeon, choosing to live it up now rather than living large later. For these readers, I have written a section at the end of the book that refers to Plan B. If this is your future path, knowing how to prepare and evolve your lifestyle later in life could be valuable. It's your choice.

However, if you prefer to be more like the Bookkeeper, this book is devoted to accumulating wealth through-out your lifetime.

> **Money Mantra:** A small amount of money saved now can turn into a large sum later that can change the course of my life.

CHOOSE YOUR FINANCIAL FUTURE:

If you want to be comfortable and financially secure for life, move on to Chapter 2: Your Twenties Advantage. If you'd rather maximize your spending now and struggle financially throughout your lifetime, skip to the end of this book and read about Financial Plan B.

Chapter 2

Your Twenties Advantage

A ONCE-IN-A-LIFETIME OPPORTUNITY

It is extremely important, especially if you are now in your twenties, that you understand the incredible power of compounding. In your twenties, time is your friend!

Compounding is simply investing money, leaving it invested, and getting a return on the original money plus all the accumulated earnings, over and over...and over again. The longer the investment time frame, the more powerful the result.

Here's an example of the twentysomething investment advantage.

Let's imagine a wealth-building contest between a twenty-year-old and a thirty-year-old.

The twenty-year-old starts with nothing saved and invests $417 per month from the time of her twentieth birthday until her thirtieth birthday. Over the course of 120 months, this is a total savings of $50,040 in ten years. The twenty-year-old never saves any additional money from age thirty but leaves her original money invested until she turns seventy.

The thirty-year-old saves $417 per month from his thirtieth birthday until his seventieth birthday—that's forty years and a total savings of $200,160. Both contestants earn an identical 8-percent investment return. So, who has the most money at age seventy?

The thirty-year-old has a respectable $1,296,318 at his age seventy, from his original investment of just over $200,000—more than a $1 million gain over a working career. Remarkably, the twenty-year-old has accumulated $1,574,827 from her total investment of just over $50,000—a gain of over $1,500,000.

The twenty-year-old scores a big win with less effort because she started saving earlier in her lifetime. Early attention to finances has incredibly powerful results in one's life.

To take it one step further, if a third saver/investor put aside money like the twentysomething, and also saved from age thirty to seventy like the thirtysomething, combining the results of the two savers in our story, that person would have saved $250,200, which would have accumulated to $2,871,145!

UNDERSTANDING COMPOUNDING

If your long-term goal is to live a bigger, more comfortable life as you mature, it is ideal to start saving and investing now. Here I provide a simple mathematical explanation.

Imagine that, *over long periods of time*, earning an 8-percent average annual return is possible by investing in a broadly diversified stock index mutual fund. Based on historical evidence, this is likely. Later I'll explain this assumption, but for the purpose of illustrating the concept here, let's use 8 percent as a reasonable long-term average yearly result.

The table below shows a one-time investment of $5,000, the length of time invested, and—earning 8 percent per year—the future value of that one investment.

ONE-TIME INITIAL INVESTMENT	TIME FRAME	VALUE AT AGE 70
Saving $5,000 at age 20	50 years	$234,508
Saving $5,000 at age 30	40 years	$108,622
Saving $5,000 at age 40	30 years	$50,313
Saving $5,000 at age 50	20 years	$23,304

In each of the time frames above, the investment is an identical $5,000. The assumed annual investment return is an identical 8 percent. The only variable is the time frame. Look at the amazing difference in end results for the early saver who makes an investment at age twenty.

Next, consider saving monthly from each of the following points in life, which are noted in the first column of the chart below, as you add $417 per month—that's just over $5,000 annually—to your $5,000 initial investment. *The saver who starts at age twenty winds up with more than double the amount of the saver who begins at age thirty!* This is the impact of compounding, a concept you should put to work immediately, or as soon as you are able.

INITIAL $5,000 INVESTMENT WITH ADDITIONS	TIME FRAME	SAVED MONTHLY	VALUE AT AGE 70
$417 monthly starting at age 20	50 years	$250,200	$3,576,921
$417 monthly starting at age 30	40 years	$200,160	$1,577,117
$417 monthly starting at age 40	30 years	$150,120	$676,158
$417 monthly starting at age 50	20 years	$100,080	$270,255

Do you see how the money you save in your twenties is worth so much more than savings put away at a later age? If you fully understand this and take the actions I propose in this book, your life savings will stack up in an impressive way. However, if you start investing later, if at all, you could end up struggling financially like many Americans. I don't want that for you.

The money you save before you are thirty years of age—and it doesn't have to be exorbitant amounts!—can make an enormous difference in your lifelong financial confidence and success. Albert Einstein famously said, "*Compound interest is the eighth wonder of the world. He who understands it, earns it; he who doesn't, pays it.*"

Twentysomething adults can put themselves into

a position to dominate the wealth-building contest, and with less financial investment, if they will only begin saving and investing now. Finding a way to save even a small amount of money early in life gives you a disproportionately greater advantage financially and personally in your later years. And I'm not implying that you'll be old and gray before you can cash in—I'm referring to the next ten, fifteen, or twenty years. You will see an amazing difference in your future for choices made now.

> **Money Mantra:** Time is on my side! Before I turn thirty, I have an incredible opportunity to take advantage of compounding interest on my money.

CHOOSE YOUR FINANCIAL FUTURE:

If you're sold on the idea of investing now while you're in your twenties, go to Chapter 3 to read about my former student, Barry the Bartender. Not sold yet? Skip to the back of the book for Financial Plan B.

Chapter 3

Barry the Bartender

START YOUR BIGGER FUTURE WITH FIVE SIMPLE STEPS

I realize it can be a challenge to save money in your twenties, but it *can* be done. Many of my former college students have reported wonderful results. Barry was a student in the personal finance class I taught at the University of Nebraska-Lincoln (UNL). He appeared less than enthused about college. He showed up for class every day but usually fell asleep sometime during the first half hour. Finally, I asked him to stick around after class to see if I could inspire him—or at least figure out why he seemed so bored during class.

Barry explained that he was very interested in personal finance and enjoyed my class, but he worked as a bartender at a local college watering hole and never got to sleep before 3:00 a.m. He had some additional odd jobs that brought in some cash, and the idea of saving and investing appealed to him. He just had trouble staying awake during my 3:30 p.m. class.

After we discussed getting him more engaged, he moved to the front of the classroom and, with my approval, regularly brought a tall, steaming coffee to keep him alert. Though not a model student grade-wise, he often discussed financial topics with me after class. He usually seemed open to my suggestions about the money he was currently accumulating.

For a couple of years, I lost track of what Barry was doing, but we remained in touch via social media. Then, one day, Barry called to request a visit with me at my office. I wondered how he was doing and, in particular, how his wealth-building plan was working out.

When he was taking my class, Barry had started aggressively saving money, paying off loans, and building cash. All he needed was a little direction. He immediately put what he learned in class to work in his life and saved much more than 10 percent of his earnings, which is what I had suggested.

At the time, he tended bar six nights a week and interned part-time for a local company. He mowed lawns in the summer, and he ran a snow removal service during the winter months. From his combined income, he funded a Roth IRA and saved up a down payment to purchase the large house where he had been renting a room. He quickly improved the house with new carpet, paint, and other home improvements, and he raised the rent of other tenants to a level that paid his mortgage.

Barry, now in his late twenties, came to me to set up an investment account for the nearly $100,000 he had saved. He wanted to commit to a long-term investment plan.

Fast-forward a few more years, and Barry is no longer a bartender. He sold his rental house and moved into a family home that he purchased. Though it took him a few extra years to graduate from college, he is a full-time employee with a local company, and maximizes his savings in an employer-provided retirement account. Barry has investment accounts and cash in the bank, and he is on his way to being a multimil-lionaire before his fortieth birthday. Best of all, Barry's story is only beginning. He has a lifetime of financial freedom and stability ahead of him.

The lesson you can learn from Barry is to start saving as early as possible, which means now. Save what you can and increase it over time.

Do not waste the incredible opportunity to save money before age thirty! Start *today* by saving some part—it can be small in the beginning—of the money you receive as earnings from work, tips you collect as a server or bartender, or cash gifts from your rich aunt or generous grandfather.

Commit now to save at least one dollar every time you handle money, and begin building from there. How do you get started? I've crafted a short list of actions—the Five Financial Foundations—that anyone can follow. By observing real people, like the Bookkeeper who intuitively applied these basic principles, I discov-ered the simple secrets to working toward building a secure financial life, while also building wealth to support current lifestyle choices and important life experiences.

THE FIVE FINANCIAL FOUNDATIONS

I developed the Five Financial Foundations over my career as a financial professional. The Five Financial Foundations are simple, making this approach to building your financial future especially useful. Anyone who really wants a bigger and better financial future can start with these critical guidelines. Below is an overview, and more details follow throughout the book.

1. SAVE SOME AMOUNT OF MONEY EVERY TIME YOU GET PAID.

If you are able, try an initial target savings rate of 10 percent of your earnings. If you are just getting started, a lesser percentage is acceptable—any savings will do. The most important factor is to begin the habit of saving money every time you get paid. Build your "savings muscles" in the same way you build physical strength. More on this is in Chapter 5: Getting Fit Financially.

2. ALWAYS HAVE A CASH RESERVE FOR EMERGENCIES AND LARGER CONSUMER GOODS PURCHASES, SUCH AS A CAR OR FURNISHINGS, TO AVOID BORROWING MONEY AND PAYING INTEREST.

This amount can vary depending on a person's situation, but an initial target is a minimum of one to two months' living expenses. Later in life, it's ideal to have a full year's living expenses held in reserve. Read in more detail about cash reserves in Chapter 7: Putting Wood in the Shed.

3. TAKE FULL ADVANTAGE OF TAX-FAVORED INVESTMENT ACCOUNTS, SUCH AS YOUR EMPLOYER'S RETIREMENT SAVINGS PLAN, AN IRA, OR A ROTH IRA.

Learn about these long-term savings vehicles through which most successful people build their largest pools of wealth. Start early in life, put money into growth investments, and let the money work for you! These investment accounts are outlined in detail in Chapter 8: Dollar-Cost Angie.

4. IF YOU DECIDE TO OWN A HOME, THE PURCHASE PRICE SHOULD BE NO MORE THAN TWICE TO TWO AND A HALF TIMES YOUR ANNUAL HOUSEHOLD INCOME.

Save and accumulate at least 20 percent of the home purchase price for a down payment, and finance the balance with a long-term fixed-rate mortgage. Unless it's really necessary, consider renting rather than buying a home until you have accumulated some savings and investments. Homeownership options are addressed in detail in Chapter 6: The Smart Housing Decision.

5. AVOID CONSUMER DEBT, WHICH IS CONSIDERED "BAD DEBT."

Bad debt is high-interest, not tax-deductible, and used to pay for things of no value or declining value, such as expensive cars, clothes and accessories, entertainment, and vacations. This is not to say you shouldn't have any of these things—it's just that you should pay cash and not borrow for them. Chapter 10: The Dangers of Debt covers more on this topic.

That's it. Pretty simple, really...but not always easy to implement. It often requires denying yourself some material items you think you need and creating new, healthy money management habits instead. Convince yourself that some things are a temporary want—if it is something you can forgo, save that money.

Saving money is simpler than it might seem to some. The basis for all self-accumulation of money starts with this formula:

SPENDING < EARNINGS

Spend less than you earn. Or find a way to earn more than you spend. This information is nothing new. It's old and timeless wisdom. To loosely quote Benjamin Franklin, there are two ways of being happy: diminish our wants or augment our means...and if you are wise, you will do both at the same time.

Many of my most financially confident and content clients started in this way, and many of my UNL students, including Barry the Bartender, have put this practice to good use. The beauty of getting started early is that it affords you more choices later in life. You want to have more money, of course, but the importance of money is not about being rich financially—it's about having a wealthy lifestyle that's right for you.

> **Money Mantra:** I can have a little fun now with my money while still socking some away for my future. I can do this; it will change my life.

CHOOSE YOUR FINANCIAL FUTURE:

If you want a bigger and better future, don't be dismayed by the title of Chapter 4: Why Money Is Not

Important. If you feel it's too hard to envision future results, skip to the back of the book for Financial Plan B.

Why Money Is Not Important

IT'S WHAT MONEY CAN DO FOR YOU THAT'S IMPORTANT

Before you get the idea that having lots of money is the only goal, let me tell you that money is *not* the only goal! Based on my non-scientific observation of clients for the last four decades, I can confidently say that obtaining wealth and making money as your main ambition can lead to as much unhappiness as having little or no money.

In the *New York Times* bestselling book *Abundance: The Future Is Better Than You Think,* authors Peter Diamandis and Steven Kotler share a study of the effect income levels have on individuals in the United States. The study concludes that the farther above or below the median income someone is, the higher the likelihood that the person will be unhappy.

In my professional career, I have certainly witnessed many people who were financially successful but led unhappy lives. Their focus was on the money and wealth rather than on what was really important to them. A wise client told me, *"Jeff, money is not important; it's what money can do for you and your family that is important."*

What can money do for you? Money can provide a safe, comfortable home and healthy living conditions. It provides proper nutrition and medical care. Some of the enjoyments and comforts of life are purchased with money. And it often takes money to provide education and support for children.

Money might give you confidence that you can be financially independent for life. And it can make it possible to switch from an unsatisfying vocation to something more interesting or exciting. It might also mean making work optional at some point during your career.

But from my viewpoint, and that of many people I have worked with over the years, what "enough" money can do for you and the people you love is most important. Warren Buffett, investor, philanthropist, and one of the richest men in the world, once told a University of Georgia audience, *"Measure your success in life by how many of the people you want to have love you actually do love you."*

Determine that if you are going to accumulate money and build wealth, it's to be financially free to care for the people you love. You can also make contributions to people, causes, and charities that are important to you. You will be able to live with confidence in your financial well-being that many people never enjoy.

Clearly identifying your goals and *why they are important to you* is the fuel that drives you to make good choices and take actions that are consistent with how you truly want to live. Through the ages, many philosophers have written on the topic of "moderation and satisfaction." Start by looking up Aristotle's Golden Mean, a 2,500-year-old principle promoting contentment and balance in life. Now might be a good time to jot down a few thoughts of your own.

WRITTEN GOALS ARE LIKE A MAGNET

One of the books in my personal "real-life master's degree" library is *Think and Grow Rich*. Get a copy and read and re-read it with a highlighter in hand. In the classic book, author Napoleon Hill states, "*Written goals are like a magnet that draws you to them*." I've found this to be absolutely true. Having worked with hundreds, perhaps thousands, of individuals in the development of their life's financial plans, I have seen the magic of putting goals in writing.

How you record your goals is unimportant, but they must be in writing. You can jot notes on index cards, journal in the pages of a notebook, or create a document saved to your tablet or desktop. Start with a simple list of what you want to happen in your life, what financial resources are necessary, and why these things are important to you. A goal identification worksheet appears at the end of this chapter, and you are free to photocopy it for use and reuse.

It is my belief that regularly reviewing and contemplating future life goals greatly increases the probability of your success. The first step in the planning process is to identify *what* you really want in life, and this requires a lot of thought. The second—and most often overlooked—step is to carefully consider *why* you want to reach these goals. After carefully considering and discovering what you want to do and why it is really important to you, the *how* of what you need to do to achieve your goals becomes much easier to accomplish.

Sometime soon, think about what is truly important to you in life—not necessarily what your parents, family members, or peers think.

> **Money Mantra:** Making money and creating wealth as my only goals are hollow ambitions. I will contemplate and determine what's really important to me.

CHOOSE YOUR FINANCIAL FUTURE:

If you feel pumped to flex your money muscles, move along to Chapter 5: Getting Fit Financially. If living your best life is not important to you, go to the back of the book for Financial Plan B.

Important Goal	Why It's Important	How Much and When	Next Step

Chapter 5

Getting Fit Financially

HOW TO BUILD YOUR SAVINGS MUSCLES

Start flexing your financial power by saving some amount of money. I've said it before, but I want to emphasize this point: it's a lot more productive if you begin saving right now.

True, some people do not have to save money to have money. They create popular music, movies, and entertainment. Or they develop software or some new process that makes life better for scores of people. They play professional sports or perform some other feat that draws large paying crowds. This could be you, too—I would never encourage you to waylay your dreams—but until you achieve your rising stardom, this is probably *not* you.

And it's just as well if this is not you, because many people who acquire money quickly and easily often do not keep it for the long term. A lot of professional athletes, movie stars, and former executives, while once on top of their financial games, now have very little or no money.

Chances are high that those who are not in the habit of saving and accumulating a small amount of money will not hold onto a large amount of money either. The money they win in the lottery, get as a signing bonus with a professional sports contract, earn from a new patent, or inherit from a rich aunt can quickly disappear.

Many people, such as the Surgeon in this book, live in very large homes and drive expensive cars but end their lives in very sparse circumstances, sometimes even having to rely on the goodwill of family or others. To avoid such a plight, develop a mindset to always save some amount of money every time you get paid or acquire any cash. Then you can live with as much certainty as is possible regarding your financial circumstances.

BUILDING YOUR SAVINGS MUSCLES

Spending less than you earn seems simple enough, but for many reasons, it can be difficult in today's world. But it can be done, and this is how to develop a successful saving habit. Learning to save money is like getting into peak physical condition. Imagine you want to get physically fit, so the first day you set out to run five miles. How do you think you would fare? Do you think you could complete a five-mile run on day one? It's not probable. More likely, you would be sore, or even injured, and unable to run again for days.

It would be better to start with a daily jog around the block. After a week, increase to two laps around the block. Gradually building up to a greater distance and longer workout leads to stronger physical conditioning. The same is true if you want to strengthen your financial condition. Rather than taking a thick slice out of your next paycheck, try saving a smaller, more manageable amount. Increase your savings from there to a more substantial goal.

How much is enough to start saving? That depends on your situation. If you're a college or high school student, start by saving from your part-time job. Are you a server or bartender? If possible, try putting away my recommended initial savings rate of 10 percent of your "take home pay." Saving 10 percent is all about adjusting your standard of living to 90 percent of your pay and banking the remainder.

Maybe all you can afford is a dollar or two every shift you work. Just begin with the largest amount you can stick with on a regular schedule. You can always increase it from there as you build your savings muscles. The greatest hurdle for many people is just getting started. So, if you're saving some amount regularly, you're on track.

If you work full time, determine an amount you can save and make that a priority. Some people give up expensive visits to the coffee shop, while others stop eating out for every meal. Take a look at your lifestyle expenses, and consider shifting to a lower gear—perhaps a less expensive car, a smaller apartment, or dialed-down shopping sprees.

As your earnings rise and expenses are under control, steadily increase your savings to 15 percent or 20 percent of your income—or whatever amount your goals require. Some prolific savers I know save more than 50 percent of their earnings!

SPEND SOME, SAVE SOME

I have always spoken out about the need to temper spending and start investing. Still, I don't believe you should only save and invest but never have any fun. It's just that I don't want you to miss the opportunity to save before age thirty. Yes, I'll say it again: don't lose the advantage of starting your savings early in life!

Many people never find the balance between spending and saving money, instead focusing only on meeting current bills and never accumulating investments. They don't prepay debts, and they don't fully fund their 401(k) plans, only investing enough to get the customary 3 percent match from employers. At this rate, chances are good they won't have enough saved to educate their children and retire comfortably. They usually have some pesky debt that doesn't get paid off, and they typically feel behind financially.

Some natural-born savers have the opposite problem. They build wealth but have trouble enjoying what money can do for them. They and their families live far below the standard of living they could enjoy. They miss opportunities to spend some of their money enjoying unique life experiences. Why not strike a balance between saving and spending your money?

FIVE CAR PURCHASES BEFORE AGE FORTY

A frequent area of excess spending is the purchase of expensive cars when a lesser-priced car works just as well. The following is my theoretical example of how a young person, like you, could have an extra $500,000 to accelerate or enhance your life when you reach retirement.

Let's assume, in this example, that an average middle-income individual might trade cars about every three or four years. Cars can be a great expense. Sure, it's fun to have a new car! Everyone loves that new car smell, right? But it can be expensive, especially if you haven't started building your net worth.

From my observation, the average college graduate or twentysomething individual could buy five cars before age forty. But high-priced cars with big payments or lease commitments, costly maintenance, and high insurance premiums can interfere with wealth building. A young person or couple should instead be investing money to compound for future growth.

Consider how you and your family could benefit if, each time you go car shopping, you make a car purchase that is $5,000 less than you can afford and put that savings to work for your future. *Instead of buying a $30,000 car, you take home a $25,000 car and bank the rest.* If you buy five cars before age forty, you are investing an additional $25,000. Doesn't seem like that much sacrifice, does it?

To me, it looks like more than *$500,000* in future assets! Look at the math behind this claim:

8% × 40 years = 21X

Money that grows for forty years at 8 percent multiplies over twenty-one times in value. Do the math! Eight percent might seem like a high return, but based on historic returns of equity markets (as represented by the Standard and Poor's 500 Index) over *forty years or greater periods* of time, a projected 8-percent average yearly gain is justified.

Assume you trade for a new or pre-owned car every three years—at age twenty-five, twenty-eight, thirty-one, thirty-four, and thirty-seven—each time purchasing a lower-priced car and investing $5,000 for the long term. Each car you buy will likely lose most of its value in a few years, but the $5,000 could grow to over $108,000 in forty years:

$$\$5{,}000 \times 8\% \times 40 \text{ years} = \$108{,}623$$

Now multiply that for the five cars you bought before age forty. You could have an additional $108,623 available at age sixty-five, sixty-eight, seventy-one, seventy-four, and seventy-seven—a grand total of $543,115!

If you desire to build wealth, and want to have a comfortable, lower-stress life, these are the kinds of actions that build your financial foundation. Going for a slightly less extravagant or snazzy car is a pretty good tradeoff. You can eventually pay cash for the luxury car, after you have created your wealth. I call this being *"frugal 'til forty, living large later."*

I am not a fun hater! But cutting back in your early earning years is smart because it puts money to work and can take off a lot of financial pressure later. I've seen it happen for decades, *so this is stuff that doesn't change with the seasons.* Cars are expensive and this expense can be controlled. The same is true for home purchases.

CHOOSE YOUR FINANCIAL FUTURE:

Starting to see the value of cutting back on lifestyle expenses and larger purchases? Move on to Chapter 6: The Smart Housing Decision to learn how you can increase wealth by cutting back on one of your largest expenditures: housing. If freeing up additional cash for investment isn't important to you right now, skip to the back of the book for Financial Plan B.

Chapter 6

The Smart Housing Decision

RIGHTSIZING YOUR CASTLE

Spending the right amount of money on your housing, especially at the start, is critical. If you can do it, consider renting a nice but not too expensive apartment. Reducing home expenses increases net cash, and this permits you to put savings in a retirement plan and build your cash reserve fund—including a large down payment for a future home purchase.

You might decide you need or want to own your house at an early age. I understand this, but it comes at a large cost if it causes you to limit your savings and prevents you from paying off loans. If you do choose to make a home purchase, consider a property that's modest and not so palatial. Read examples A and B below, which outline reasonable expectations of home costs in two contrasting scenarios:

HOMEOWNERSHIP OPTION A

You want a nice house right now, and you figure it will save you from having to move to a better family home in the future. Plus, you hear that the mortgage interest is a tax shelter and buying a home gives you equity buildup. Who wants to waste money on rent, anyway? Plus, you want that house! So, with some family help, you take on all the home mortgage for which you can qualify.

Home Purchase Price	$400,000
20% Down Payment (from savings, family loan, or second mortgage loan)	$80,000
Your Mortgage Loan	$320,000

MONTHLY EXPENSES

Mortgage Payment (principal plus 4% interest for a thirty-year term)	$1,527.73
Property Tax Escrow (calculated annually at 2% of assessed home value)	$666.67
Homeowners Insurance Premium	$405.60
Total Monthly Principal, Interest, Property Tax, and Insurance (PITI)	$2,600

In addition to the mortgage payment, which often includes the collection of property taxes and insurance as shown here, there are other considerable expenses. Furnishing the home, decorating, landscaping, and yard care are all examples of significant costs. The larger the home, the greater these additional expenses can be.

HOMEOWNERSHIP OPTION B

You need or want a house but are willing to choose a more affordable and manageable home. You don't need a palatial place to live. The bank might even qualify you for a hefty home loan, but why stretch your housing expenses to the max? You prefer to be comfortable now and live large later in life after the financial wind is at your back.

Home Purchase Price	$250,000
20% Down Payment	$50,000
Your Mortgage Loan	$200,000

MONTHLY EXPENSES

Mortgage Payment (principal plus 4% interest for a thirty-year term)	$954.83
Property Tax Escrow (calculated annually at 2% of assessed value)	$416.67
Homeowners Insurance Premium	$228.50
Total Monthly Principal, Interest, Property Tax, and Insurance (PITI)	$1,600

Homeownership Option B requires a $30,000 lower down payment. That extra cash, if available to you, can be invested instead or used to pay off loans. Option B also comes with $1,000 less in monthly expenses—that's $12,000 per year!—that can be used for wealth building. Plus, all related household expenses could be higher for the more expensive home in Homeownership Option A, including steeper property taxes, more furniture, a larger yard, more repairs, and more upkeep.

When you consider buying a home, here's the guideline I learned from clients who were wealth builders:

RIGHTSIZE YOUR CASTLE AT TWO AND A HALF TIMES YOUR HOUSEHOLD INCOME (OR LESS)

Let me be clear on a couple of things right away. Deductible mortgage interest can reduce your income tax bill. Yes, the deductibility makes homeownership seem more attractive. But *when does spending one dollar in interest to save you thirty cents or forty cents ever make you money?*

If you have a $200,000 mortgage at 4 percent interest, you will pay approximately $8,000 in tax-deductible interest. If you file an itemized return, this interest may be used to reduce your taxable income, and if you are in a 30 percent marginal tax bracket, you get $2,400 of reduced tax due. But you still paid a net payment of $5,600 in interest plus principal. This assumes you itemize your expenses. If you claim the standard deduction, which is presently $12,500 per person, you get this deduction whether you have mortgage interest or are paying rent.

Get to know a great certified public accountant (CPA) or other tax professional who can help you understand and implement tax-wise strategies.

Homeownership does not always equate to equity

buildup either. Yes, investing in your home can at times build wealth, especially if you live in your house for many years. But it can also result in a loss of capital.

For example, say you buy the modest home in Home-ownership Option B. You pay $250,000, which is about twice your household take-home pay—either yours alone, or yours combined with your domestic partner's income. Then perhaps you are offered a great career opportunity a couple of years later, and it requires a move to a new city. Or maybe your income increases substantially and, at the same time, you're expecting twins so you need a bigger house.

So, you decide to put your home on the market. After making payments for two years, the principal has been paid down slightly, but in the early years of a mortgage, payments are applied mostly to interest and very little is credited to principal reduction. In this example, about $7,500 of the $250,000 mortgage would have been paid off during the period you owned the house. Equity buildup? Not so much.

You call your real estate agent and list the home for sale. The market appraisal of your home has gone up $10,000 in value, so it is listed at $260,000. Within a short time, you accept an offer for the full asking price. More equity buildup? Nope, not necessarily.

You paid $50,000 down, paid a few thousand dollars off the mortgage principal, and sold the house for a profit. But at closing, you receive a check for less than the original $50,000 you paid as a down payment. This is due to closing costs, including the real estate company's 7 percent commission fee charged for selling the home.

Sale Price	$260,000
7% Commission	-$18,200
Closing Costs	-$2,500
Net Sale	$239,300
Estimated Loan Payoff	-$192,500
Your Check at Closing	$46,800

So, here's the hard truth about equity buildup: unless you are in a very rapidly rising home market or plan to stay in the home for a long time—five years minimum and hopefully longer—do not expect to build much equity.

If you choose instead to rent an apartment, your rent is likely lower than a mortgage payment, property taxes, homeowners' insurance, and the related costs of homeownership. The savings of renting versus buying a house could go into savings, a retirement plan, or paying off debt. And don't forget the $50,000 down payment that could have been held in savings, invested, or used to pay off your education loans.

Renting until you're more financially stable is a different kind of equity buildup and might be a better path for some than buying a home too soon or purchasing one that pushes you to your qualifying limit.

> **Money Mantra:** I can live comfortably and start building wealth at the same time by making the smart housing decision.

CHOOSE YOUR FINANCIAL FUTURE:

Feeling financially strong and ready to start saving? Move on to Chapter 7: Putting Wood in the Shed. Do you believe building a cash reserve is unimportant? Head to the back of the book for Financial Plan B.

Chapter 7

Putting Wood in the Shed

REDUCING LIFE'S
FINANCIAL PRESSURES

On the Nebraska farm where I was raised, to heat the house during the cold winter months, my ancestors had to prepare by accumulating wood and other materials during the hot summer months.

When I think about building a cash reserve, I think of it as *"putting wood in the shed."* Back in the day, it was necessary to save during the summer because winter soon followed. In building a cash reserve, it's sometimes difficult to set aside cash for an undefined, unknown future need—especially when there are so many other opportunities to spend it!

Everyone can benefit from building a cash reserve for future unplanned emergency expenses. Having money stashed away takes the pressure out of life. In addition to having a "just in case" fund, it's smart to plan for larger purchases such as a car, a down payment on a home, or a family vacation.

Yet many Americans do not have any meaningful amounts of cash available. This forces some to take financial actions that are not ideal, such as high-interest loans that linger for years. Such a loan might cost the borrower more in interest than the original loan principal. For young adults, low or no cash reserve might mean relying on parents or other family members to help, which could strain family relationships. Lack of cash might even require the forced sale of potentially valuable assets or investments prematurely. It also can lead to missed opportunities.

Without a cash reserve, financial confidence is lacking.

How much cash is enough? Deciding how much cash should be on reserve is often more of an art than a science, but this is my formula for someone who is just starting out or has never saved money: build up one to two months of living expenses as quickly as you can. As you save more in retirement plans and pay off debts, increase your cash reserve.

Not sure how to determine your monthly expenses? Here's what I suggest for my college students or recent graduates who don't always have a good handle on their living costs.

Target 10 percent of your paycheck for the next year as an amount to get started. Let's assume you make $50,000 after deductions or anticipate this as your starting salary in a future position in your intended career. Make a $5,000 cash reserve your initial goal. As your financial situation improves, bump up your reserve to six months of living expenses. Add amounts accordingly for large purchases you plan to make in the next year or two.

Later in life or in retirement, the amount of cash reserve should be twelve months of known living expenses plus any future potential large purchases or expenditures. It requires some discipline and a desire to get ahead to build up a cash reserve. But the choice to be a little thrifty or frugal is a decision to trade a spendy "live for the moment" lifestyle for a secure life for yourself and the people most important to you.

To be clear, this means forgoing the momentary pleasure of purchasing some unnecessary or frivolous material goods. In return, you will eventually live a very comfortable life with financial confidence. The accomplished saver learns to build cash and to pre-plan for all large expenditures in addition to having an emergency fund on reserve.

Your cash reserve should be held in a secure account with instant liquidity and no volatility in price, such as a bank savings account or money market account. While some interest or return is desirable, strictly avoid exchanging certainty for a higher interest rate.

In an accessible reserve fund, your cash will probably not generate earnings anywhere near the return of your long-term growth investment accounts over time. But the reserve fund will make you money in the form of not paying interest on high-cost emergency loans or investments sold at the wrong time. Having a cash reserve allows you to leave long-term investments untouched during market pullbacks. Having cash reserves makes it possible to hold on for the long pull which could eventually return much more than the interest on a money fund.

For those of us who don't have much of a shot at inventing new software, acting in feature films, or playing professional basketball, measured spending and deliberate lifestyle choices are a must.

IT DOESN'T MATTER WHAT OTHERS THINK

If you choose to ignore what other people think about your financial situation, you'll be in a much better mindset. Many people make life-changing decisions because of how they believe their social group or family members might perceive them.

The price for making unnecessarily lofty purchases and living an escalating lifestyle? You forgo the calm and confidence that goes with having lower fixed costs and a reasonable cash reserve. Stretching your budget to the limits can put a lot of strain on a marriage and other relationships. Being strapped for cash is no way to live.

Maybe you can identify people you know who have lived way beyond their means and needed to develop a Plan B. It might also be obvious to you the other people you know who were financially savvy.

> **Money Mantra:** Having cash gives me financial control and confidence. Financially confident people manage their money so it's liquid, not leveraged.

CHOOSE YOUR FINANCIAL FUTURE:

You're convinced that saving is the way to go—it's time to turn your attention to long-term growth investments, so go to the next chapter. Um, you're convinced you are doomed because you have no financial savvy? You, too, should read on to Chapter 8. Meet Dollar-Cost Angie, who says, *"I'm not good with money."*

Chapter 8

Dollar-Cost Angie: "I'm Not Good with Money"

BUILDING YOUR BIGGEST PILE OF MONEY

Angie, a friend of a friend, called me for financial advice in the early 1980s, saying, "I'm not good with money and could use some help." I was a rookie stockbroker, sitting at my desk and "dialing for dollars," trying to find new clients who had money to invest. Frankly, I didn't know all that much about financial planning.

But I did know more than Angie did, and I was glad to offer advice by phone, even if she didn't have enough money to be a client. Angie had just gotten "a real job," after waitressing and doing other part-time jobs while completing her college degree. Her employer had just adopted a 401(k) retirement savings plan, and she had no idea how much to save or how to invest the money.

After some discussion with me, she decided to save a small amount each paycheck into the 401(k). Her employer's payroll department would deduct it before she received her take-home pay, and she felt that saving this way was a good idea because she wasn't "good with money." I helped her choose one of the investment options offered by the plan, a mutual fund from a well-known mutual fund company.

About five years later, Angie called me. I hadn't spoken to her since our first telephone call. She wanted to come to my office and show me her retirement savings plan statement. Something was wrong, she told me—the statement didn't look right to her. We arranged for a quick meeting at my office, and I discovered to her surprise and mine that the value of the account was over $20,000. She said this was too much money and that there must be a mistake! But the statement was correct.

Angie had started saving a set amount and increased the amount each year when she got a pay raise. She hadn't changed the original mutual fund investment. It was now worth a fair amount more than what she had invested during the few years since we had talked. Angie never became a client, and we didn't stay in touch. But I heard from her recently, and she never saved any other money but continued to participate with contributions to the retirement plan. She spent most of her earnings on clothes, purses, new cars, vacations, and other desires.

But she always stayed enrolled in the retirement plan and never touched that money. It remained invested through the ups and downs of the last forty years. She didn't pay much attention to the account because, again she told me, "I'm not good with money."

The power of dollar-cost averaging (DCA) over the years is immense! This is what Angie unwittingly did over the course of four decades. By investing steadily through up and down markets, she was buying more shares during "down" markets and fewer shares when the stock market was strong. She was building her holdings at an attractive average price. It worked especially well for her because she left it untouched to work for her.

Dollar-cost averaging (DCA) is a simple strategy of investing a set amount at set intervals. For example, $500 every two weeks. When markets rise, fewer shares are purchased; when market values decline, more shares are purchased at the lower price. Over time it can lead to the acquisition of shares at an attractive "average" price.

Today, *Dollar-Cost Angie*, as I think of her, is retiring with over $2 million in her plan. She happily spent everything else she earned and plans to collect Social Security retirement at a reduced level at age sixty-two. I advised her to wait to file for Social Security later, because the monthly amount will be higher for life if she delays collecting benefits until her full retirement age of sixty-seven. She laughed and said she didn't care; she wanted the extra check right now. She acknowledged that delaying is probably the right thing to do but again stated, "I'm not very good with money."

What you need to understand about Angie's story is the power of three things she applied to her financial situation and, with only minor adjustments, let it work for her.

1. Angie got started early in life so her money could work for her for a long time. It's that compounding thing!

2. She harnessed the power of investing in ownership investments, such as a stock index mutual fund.
3. Angie took the opportunity to avoid or delay income taxes by using tax-advantaged retirement accounts.

TAX-ADVANTAGED RETIREMENT ACCOUNTS

This is where most working people build up their largest investment accounts. You have probably heard the terms "IRA," "Roth IRA," and "401(k)" and know what these investment tools are and how they work. But you may not know everything you need to know about these incredible wealth-building accounts. *Following is a general overview of retirement accounts. Before investing, do more research or work with a professional who can assist you in navigating the rules.*

TRADITIONAL IRA

IRA is an acronym for individual retirement account. Internal Revenue Service materials often refer to it as an individual retirement arrangement. These are the basics of a *traditional IRA*: You put money into this account, and the contribution is *tax-deductible*.

The contribution lowers your taxable income and therefore reduces your tax payment in the year of contribution. This is the first tax advantage. Note that there are some requirements you must meet to be eligible to make a deductible contribution. If you participate in your employer's retirement plan and have an income higher than an annually determined level, you may not be eligible to make a deductible contribution to a traditional IRA.

Because of the income tax deduction, it reduces the amount of out-of-pocket contribution you must make. Say you deposited $6,000, the maximum allowed contribution for 2022, in your new IRA and that you are in a 20 percent income tax bracket. The $6,000 deduction reduces your income tax by $1,200 that year. Your net out-of-pocket cost after tax is $4,800, but you have $6,000 that goes to work and can remain invested for many years!

Then, you invest the money in the IRA based on offerings of the financial institution that is the custodian that holds this money for you. If you set up your IRA with your bank, you probably will invest in an interest-bearing certificate or other savings account with the bank. If you invest with a mutual fund company, you will likely be able to choose from many mutual funds offered by that company. If you set up your IRA with a stock brokerage firm, you could have a wide range of stocks, bonds, annuities, and mutual funds as investment choices for your IRA.

You might want to hire professional help, and that is covered in Chapter 13: The Sea Captain and the Golf Professional.

The interest or gains in this IRA are not currently taxable, which is why retirement accounts are often referred to as tax-deferred accounts. This is a second and very important advantage. There is also a drawback, however. If you withdraw money from this account before age fifty-nine and a half, you must pay tax on the withdrawal plus a 10 percent penalty. Money you put into an IRA is meant to be a long-term investment that you should not need to touch until your retirement years. Some exceptions allow for a penalty-free early withdrawal. When you quit working, the money that has accumulated is then taxable as it is withdrawn.

ROTH IRA

The *Roth IRA* is very similar to...and very different than a traditional IRA. It's set up just like the traditional IRA, and investors can make annual contributions of up to $6,000 into a Roth IRA. However, the contribution is *not* deductible for tax purposes. The accumulated earnings inside the account grow without current taxation. But when you withdraw money from the Roth at retirement, there are *no income taxes on the original contribution or the years of accumulated earnings from interest, growth, dividends, and so on.*

This can be very attractive for young investors who are not in highly taxable situations. The tax deduction may be relatively unimportant to them and the money can then be left to multiply for many years in growth investments.

To summarize, in some ways a traditional IRA and Roth IRA are opposites. Traditional IRA contributions are tax-deductible, while Roth IRA contributions are *not* deductible. Traditional withdrawals are fully taxable, while Roth withdrawals are generally not taxable.

401(K) PLAN

Some employers offer a *401(k) plan* as an employee benefit. With an IRA, you set up your account and write a check or transfer money to the sponsor institution of your choice. The 401(k) is set up by the company, and your contributions are made through paycheck deductions. It's a great way to save because it goes into retirement investments before you can even be tempted to squander it! Typically, the investment choices are available as a menu of multiple mutual fund accounts from which you can select. This is covered in more detail in Chapter 11: Scoring Your First $1 Million.

The term "401(k)" comes from the section in the Internal Revenue Code that authorizes this type of retirement savings account. The 401(k) maximum contribution for 2022 is $20,500, plus an additional $6,500 "catch-up" contribution for plan participants over age fifty. The maximum contribution limits are updated annually. If you want to maximize retirement savings in 2022, put away $6,000 in an IRA and $20,500 in a 401(k) for a total of $26,500 per year—and up to $33,000 if you are age fifty or older and IRA eligible. Remember that the amount you save is for retirement, so early withdrawals are usually subject to penalties.

However, company plans often have a loan provision through which an employee can borrow money from their plan to meet a need, usually up to $50,000. You can pay this loan back to yourself with interest. The 401(k) plan can be pre-tax like a traditional IRA—actually it is a reduction of your taxable income from your employer and not a deduction—or it can be an after-tax contribution like a Roth IRA if your company plan provisions allow after-tax contributions.

What happens when you leave the employer where you have the 401(k) account? Do not take the cash in a check as many do, since it's taxable and subject to that nasty 10 percent penalty! You can normally choose to leave it with the former employer, or you can transfer it tax-free into your new company 401(k) plan or to an IRA that you set up. Sounds simple, but you might want to engage professional help in getting this done properly.

This is a very general overview intended to help you begin using these very important types of tax-advantaged accounts. Retirement accounts are a good start to a steady savings plan, if you contribute every time you get a check and enjoy tax advantages while saving. *I took my own advice on this one.*

MY BIGGEST POOL OF MONEY

Since I entered the investment business shortly after college, I got comfortable with the idea of just leaving my money invested in stocks. That's not the case for everyone, depending on risk tolerance, stage of life, and other specific individual or financial circumstances. Yes, my investments fluctuated...a lot! But I stayed invested through some scary market events and enjoyed nice gains during some big rising markets. I have no clear way to calculate the true return, but it's probably been a market-like return. My investments probably gained something either side of 10 percent on average since the early 1980s. Please note that this return isn't indicative of future performance.

But after forty years in the workforce, my largest pool of investment money is in retirement accounts: my IRA and 401(k). This is true for most people who make a living by working for someone else. Here are the reasons:

- One hundred percent of the money saved to the account (income taxes are not withheld from contributions) gets invested and put to work. Granted, this money will be taxed, but the money I saved in my twenties won't get taxed until withdrawals start after I retire or when I'm required to take money out at age seventy-two.

- The growth, the dividends, the interest, and all the returns compound without taxation until they're withdrawn. I haven't retired yet, so the money that is growing has never been taxed. Woo-hoo!

- Because there is a 10 percent penalty if I were to withdraw funds prematurely, I never spent any of the money. I left it invested, even though I was less than frugal with some of the non-retirement account money I accumulated.

- Since I always maximized my contributions as I progressed in my career, I was able to take advantage of larger and larger contribution opportunities.

Though I did divide the money in the account due to divorce, and some ugly markets cut the value significantly (you probably weren't even born in 1987, but perhaps you remember the financial crisis of 2008 and the pandemic scare of 2020), it is a substantial amount that will be valuable if I quit working. Any residual amount—the money left after I kick off—can be withdrawn by my beneficiaries. Beneficiaries can withdraw the funds in a lump sum, fully taxable, or take the money over a ten-year period, spreading out the income and the taxes on the money.

It worked for me and for Dollar-Cost Angie, as well as hundreds, perhaps thousands, of people I have known and advised over the last forty years.

> **Money Mantra:** Investing early in a retirement fund doesn't guarantee immediate profits, but it could be my largest chunk of money later in life.

CHOOSE YOUR FINANCIAL FUTURE:

You're not flashy, so you're fine with saving and investing early in life. Or maybe you like to show off and prefer the immediate appearance of wealth. Either way, read about Danny and Annie in Chapter 8. Sometimes the people who seem wealthy are anything but financially well off.

Chapter 9

Danny and Annie

THE HIGH COST OF TOO MUCH TOO SOON

Danny and I met several years ago. We were matched together at the golf club where we were both members and met on the first tee late on a weekday afternoon. Walking together as we played nine holes before dinner, we got to know each other. Danny was the plant manager for a nationally known company that has a local presence in our town. His wife, Annie, was a full-time mom and homemaker.

Danny was a very skilled golfer and a nice guy. Over a refreshment after golfing, he asked me about my work. I explained what I do for clients, and he inquired about meeting with me to review his financial situation. Though he didn't come right out and say it, I got the impression he was looking to me for that financial confidence I always tout.

A couple of weeks later, we met for lunch to review Danny and Annie's financial circumstances. Here's what I discovered: Danny and Annie were in their mid-forties and had never worked with a financial planner or professional wealth advisor. Well-educated, they thought they could manage their money without paying for professional advice. They had a handful of stocks in an account they inherited some years before, but they hadn't paid too much attention to it.

Danny had attended a nationally known university, earning a bachelor's degree as well as a master's degree in engineering. While obtaining his MBA, he met Annie, a graduate school classmate. They had both worked in their careers until their two children came along. Annie had taken a few years out of the workforce to be a full-time mom, and now with the children in their teens, she was returning to work part time. Danny earned $160,000 per year plus bonuses and a generous benefits package. Annie was returning to the workforce at an anticipated part-time pay of $40,000 per year.

The couple owned a new home in the very best part

of the city. They had purchased the house for $800,000. They had a significant mortgage with a large monthly payment that included property taxes and homeowners' insurance. They enjoyed this home and felt they were getting equity buildup despite the very large monthly payment. To furnish and decorate this lovely, large home they had spent quite a lot of money and incurred some monthly payments to the furniture store and an interior decorator.

Danny was saving 6 percent of his salary in his company retirement account, and the first 6 percent saved was matched 50 percent by his company. The balance in this 401(k) account was $30,000. Danny also had a balance in a 401(k) with his former employer that was in a money fund option and valued at $200,000. Annie had an IRA valued at $8,000, which she had accumulated in a 401(k) plan from her previous employer and had rolled over to an IRA when she left the company.

They had a self-managed brokerage account with $25,000 in stocks. Their last transaction had been several years ago. They had three cash reserve accounts that totaled $14,000. And they had two education funding accounts totaling $7,000. When asked about future goals, they said a priority was to help their children get a high-quality education at a prestigious university.

Danny and Annie owned two new imported cars for which the combined monthly payments were more than $1,000. They had credit card debts and some consumer purchase debts that totaled almost $40,000.

The two were happy with their careers but felt they were always struggling despite having a good income. *Is something missing? Maybe everyone feels like this?* They weren't entirely confident and wanted my opinion on where they stood and what actions they should take, if any. In addition to educating their children, they had other hopes such as a second home or an early retirement for Danny.

I asked why they weren't investing more money or paying off debts and loans. They said they simply didn't have any extra money after paying bills. It made them both uncomfortable to share that the financial discord had created tension in their marriage.

For a moment, you be the financial planner and think about their situation and how they're doing. What changes would you recommend they make? Take a brief look at how they are doing based on the Five Financial Foundations:

1. **Save some amount of money.** How much are they saving from income?
2. **Always have a cash reserve.** What was their cash reserve for emergencies and large future purchases? How does their reserve compare to the short-term debt they have?
3. **Take full advantage of retirement accounts.** Are they fully funding their retirement plans? And how are they doing on their stated goal of saving for college for their children?
4. **Purchase a home at the right price.** Was their home appropriately priced for them based on their income?
5. **Avoid consumer debt.** Do they have high-interest loans or credit card debt?

EVALUATION AND SUGGESTIONS FOR DANNY AND ANNIE

As you can see, having a good-paying career and solid education is no guarantee of financial savvy. Are they saving? Well, yes, but only 6 percent of Danny's salary, just enough to get the employer's matching contribution. As you know, I always suggest investing at least 10 percent of income, but in this case, a fortysomething executive should be saving more.

Do they have a cash reserve? Not really, if you consider the total $14,000 in reserve and compare it to the short-term debts that total nearly $40,000. What would Danny and Annie do if they were to have an emergency or unexpected expense? They would have to borrow money.

Is Danny fully funding retirement accounts? Approaching mid-career, does Danny have a good start on an early retirement? Not necessarily. Danny could have been putting twice as much in his 401(k) account, as well as funding IRA accounts for himself and Annie. Danny did have $200,000 in a 401(k) but it was invested in a money fund, a great investment for a cash reserve purposes but not optimal for a long-term investment within a retirement account.

Now, let's take a look at the house. Is it the right size, right price? Much of their cash flow was going into the house to make the steep monthly payments of combined principal, interest, property taxes, and homeowners' insurance. Based on their income, rather than choosing an $800,000 house, a home in the $400,000 to $500,000 range would have been preferable and given them some breathing room.

Last, do they have consumer debt? Yes, they do, most of it associated with their large home and expensive cars. Their Plan B wasn't without some pain, but much better discovered at age forty than at retirement, which was the circumstance for the Surgeon.

By cutting expenses related to the home and cars, and reducing spending on entertainment, they were about to get on track. When their children went to college, they downsized from the large house to a home with a price and size appropriate for their income. They traded the expensive cars for nice mid-size cars for which they paid cash.

They built a cash reserve, and they increased retirement and education savings. Though an early retirement is unlikely, they made difficult changes and have a lower-stress situation.

> **Money Mantra:** If some people had known what I now know in my twenties, their money would look so much different today. I am choosing financial health and wealth for myself.

CHOOSE YOUR FINANCIAL FUTURE:

If you don't want to be buried under a mound of debt, read Chapter 10: The Dangers of Debt at your leisure. If you're just dying to rough up the credit limit on your new platinum card, turn as quickly as possible to Chapter 10.

Chapter 10

The Dangers of Debt: The Surgeon's Son

IS THERE SUCH A THING AS GOOD DEBT?

The thrifty Bookkeeper accumulated a significant sum and lived a comfortable life. The highly paid Surgeon ended his career financially shortchanged for retirement. The Surgeon, a really terrific professional, a high earner, and an overall great person who was very charitable, just spent too much money without investing. Unfortunately, money habits sometimes transfer from generation to generation.

Happily, many children of people like the Bookkeeper are armed with a sense of value and thriftiness that allows them to establish their own wealth-building ways while enjoying a comfortable and stress-reduced lifestyle.

After I had assisted the Surgeon in rightsizing his financial life, making sure he and his wife would have income for life after some very difficult Plan B decisions, his son asked him for a loan. When the Surgeon sought my advice about this, I told him he must say no, and I volunteered to meet with his son.

On the day of the appointment, the Surgeon's son and his wife met me at my office. We made a list of all their assets and liabilities, and created a simple net worth statement. We discovered his net worth was a *negative $200,000*! In other words, he had $200,000 more in debts and liabilities than he had in assets. And several pressing bills were due. We discussed the option of filing for bankruptcy. This was a smart, educated man with graduate degrees, high earnings, and many talents, but he was living the showy lifestyle he had learned growing up with his dad. To their credit, the couple decided they had the ability to pay off their debts and would not file for bankruptcy.

My guidance was much the same as I had suggested for his parents, but this time it was sooner in life by about twenty-five years. The choices were difficult, with a drastic reduction of expenses. I recommended trading off expensive luxury cars, slashing entertainment and dining expenses, and eliminating club memberships. The couple's children were moved from private prep schools to public education, so they could afford to attend college in the future.

Eventually, they rightsized their home, selling their fully mortgaged house in an iconic neighborhood and buying a nice smaller house that was more afford-able. Additionally, the wife, trained in a professional career but not working, returned to the workforce even though she really did not want to work. This was a drastic change in lifestyle and social standing but a necessary turnaround, which they eventually were able to achieve.

Aside from the overriding message in this book, which is to start saving early, a couple of lessons can be learned from the Surgeon's son:

1. Money management habits can be transferred from generation to generation. But if your parents or mentors aren't the best money managers, you can choose differently.

2. It is sometimes possible to correct your financial situation even at mid-career or at retirement, but there are usually consequences such as adjusting to a less extravagant lifestyle.

The Surgeon's son, like many in modern America, fell deep into a debt hole, and it took a decade for him and his family to climb out of that hole. I am not suggesting you should never borrow money. That would be nice, but it's probably not practical for most of us. That being reality, it's important to understand the difference between good debt and bad debt.

GOOD DEBT VS. BAD DEBT

Good debt is used to buy something of value that will increase in price (such as a home or other real estate investment), provide income (a business, for example), or somehow create more value than the cost of the interest charged, such as money borrowed for education or specialized training. Good debt is usually lower cost because it is well secured with valuable assets. The interest is often tax-deductible, reducing the net cost of the loan.

Bad debt is the opposite. It is used to buy something of

declining value or no value at all, such as financing a furniture purchase or using a credit card to pay for an exotic vacation. The interest is often high because the security is thin or nonexistent, and that steep interest is rarely tax-deductible. One of the most common types of bad debt is excessive credit card balances.

THE CREDIT CARD TRAP

How does a person like the Surgeon's son get so buried in debt? Unfortunately, it happens all the time and can have a major financial consequence for life. Periodically a client asks me to sit down with a son, daughter, or grandchild to "talk about money" and give some advice. I sometimes discover a great big, growing credit card balance. How the heck does that happen?

If you're a graduating college student, or just starting to earn money, your name might be on a marketing or mailing list for a financial institution. The financial institution has services and products to offer that are a valuable part of American life, and it wants you as a customer. One day you get a mailing that offers you a special rate on a new card due to your increasing credit standing. You sign up, and the card arrives a few weeks later. You get an initial $250 spending limit.

You use the card to make a purchase or two, and when the bill is due the following month, you pay it off. You do this for a few months, maybe even for a year or two. It's convenient, and you pay no interest charges because you pay in full every month. No problem so far, right? In fact, because you've been so responsible, the card company boosts your credit limit to $1,000.

Then let's say you get a new job offer and move to a new apartment in a new town. You need to buy new stuff for your new home, and you need some new clothes for work. You spend some money traveling to and from home while you adjust to your new life. You can't fully pay the card off, but you make a partial payment. No big deal, or so you think.

But you still need more new items, so you maximize your card limit again the next month, and the month after, still making payments. And you are now paying interest, not that much in actual dollar amounts, or so it seems, but at 18 percent annually. This continues, and because you are an active borrower—and now becoming a profitable customer—the credit card company expands your limit to $2,000. Congratulations, you have good credit! It is, of course, ideal to have a good credit standing, but the credit card trap comes at a cost.

Within a year or two, you might reach your spending limit almost every month, sometimes paying some principal and sometimes paying only the minimum monthly amount due. You are falling behind, but you are a great customer for the card company and guess what—they increase your limit to $5,000. Congratulations! About this time, other credit card issuers send offers of new additional credit cards that can be yours if you will only sign up.

This can go on and on for years. I've met young people with mountains of accumulated debts, sometimes large balances on more than one card. Instead of having $75,000 saved by age thirty, they might have $75,000 in debt that costs them 18 percent interest or more!

The Surgeon's son had more than a dozen cards with maximum balances. In today's world, it is necessary to have credit cards to make online purchases, to rent cars, and for other conveniences. But being intentional about always paying off the entire balance is of absolute importance.

WHEN YOU ARE IN TROUBLE

Carrying any debt over from month to month is the way trouble starts brewing. When you cannot pay the entire balance of your credit card (or cards), the warning bell should sound because you are falling into the credit card trap.

All credit card debt that is not paid off in full each month is considered bad debt. No credit card issuer will ever tell you when you are in trouble. This is how they make money, at your expense. If you cannot pay off your card balance, stop using the card until it is fully paid off. It's that simple.

What about college and other education debt? It might be good debt; it might be bad debt.

Has the education created value for you? Did it lead you to greater income potential or access to a field that requires a specific education? Were the loans processed at competitive rates? If so, the loan could be considered good debt. College loans for undirected courses of study that provide no opportunities or valuable skills could be bad debt.

> **Money Mantra:** Why borrow when I don't have to? Bad debt, particularly the credit card trap, will work against me every time. That's why I only spend money I have.

CHOOSE YOUR FINANCIAL FUTURE:

If you want to be a millionaire, move on to Chapter 11: Scoring Your First $1 Million. Um, if you're fine settling for less, cut to the back of the book for Financial Plan B.

Scoring Your First $1 Million

EASIER THAN YOU THINK... IF YOU START EARLY

Multimillionaires will tell you that getting the first $1 million is the hardest. The next $1 million is easier, and the $1 million after that is easier yet. For now, just focus on the first! How long will it take you to accumulate your first $1 million balance? How much will you need to save monthly to reach this first goal?

The charts below demonstrate what I advocate throughout this book. There is no substitute for starting early in life. It's a combination of time and rate of return and the amount invested. You have various levels of control over all three of these elements. Do you control when you get started and how long you can invest? Yes, you do, and now is the time. Do you control the amounts you invest or contribute? Yes, you do. A steady, long-term plan will likely yield a better result than sporadic investing.

Do you control your investment return? Well, not in the short term if you own stocks or stock mutual funds. But over decades, you could realize something near the historical return in stocks. A little research into the history of the Standard and Poor's 500 Index and you will discover average annual returns in the range of 10 percent when looking at thirty- and forty-year periods. And you can control your willingness to remain invested through the ups and downs of the market, even for an entire working career. For our purposes, I am going to be conservative and assume an 8 percent long-term result. This gives you lots of room to make mistakes and still reach your goal.

Let's look at a few scenarios.

A NEW GRADUATE

Let's say you're twenty-one years old, just graduated from college—or just got out of the military, or are a high school graduate with full-time employment—and you are going to start saving for the distant future. If you start saving $250 per month and earning a level 8 percent yearly, you will reach your first $1 million at age sixty-three, which is just in time for retirement. A little less than $10 per day totals $125,000, which, invested over five hundred months, becomes $1 million.

However, let's assume you can save a little more. The following chart demonstrates when those monthly payments will bring your account up to $1 million:

STARTING AT AGE 21 (ANNUAL COMPOUNDING AT 8% PER YEAR)

MONTHLY AMOUNT	AVERAGE DAILY INVESTMENT	AGE WHEN YOU REACH $1 MILLION
$250	< $10 per day	63
$600	$20 per day	52
$1,000	$33 per day	47

Here's the beauty of getting to that first $1 million before age fifty. If left invested at 8 percent, this first $1 million account more than triples in fifteen years with no additional investment. And there are plenty of years from age forty-seven to mid-sixties to save even larger sums. Of course, over time the amount you save will change. Sometimes you might have to reduce your savings or stop altogether. But you might be able to regularly increase your savings throughout your working career.

What happens if you delay just ten years, live it up in your twenties, and start saving at age thirty-one? How does that compare with the results above? Unfortunately, we don't see any $1 million returns for similar investments made by individuals who start saving in their thirties:

STARTING AT AGE 31 (ANNUAL COMPOUNDING AT 8% PER YEAR)

MONTHLY AMOUNT	BY THIS AGE	AMOUNT
$250	63	$443,489
$600	52	$390,215
$1,000	47	$387,209

Consider the fate of the late starter who has saved little or no money by mid-career. Sadly, this describes many Americans. Let's assume a fifty-year-old has saved $50,000 toward that first $1 million goal. How much would that person need to save to reach $1 million by age sixty if we assume the same 8-percent constant return?

The answer is $4,860 per month.

You control when you start saving, the length of your savings and investing period, and the amount you save. You also have some control over the return, especially over long periods of time.

LONG-TERM INVESTING IN STOCK MUTUAL FUNDS

Investing in stocks is simple. But it's not necessarily easy. It's simple because today's low-cost, well-diversified, and tax-efficient mutual fund offerings make investing uncomplicated and straightforward. But it's not so easy because of the constant attention by mass media—24/7 information access to prices via the internet or a mobile phone app. Watching the market move makes it a challenge to be patient, to maintain long-term thinking.

It's especially challenging to watch market values drop dramatically, which can and will happen over the years. Market watchers often get scared, choosing to sell at times when they should be buying. For the most part, the long-term twentysomething investor should ignore the stock market's ups and downs. Sometimes the media and other talking heads indicate that you should be making decisions to enhance your returns. This is not true—lots of buying and selling activity is *not* ideal.

HOW TO OPEN THOSE FIRST ACCOUNTS

As detailed in Chapter 8, there are three main account types in which you can invest—your employer's 401(k), an IRA you set up for yourself, or a personal non-IRA, taxable account. A good first investment choice for any of these accounts might be a stock index mutual fund with a portfolio of hundreds or even thousands of individual stock holdings. An index fund of the Standard and Poor's 500 stocks is a commonly owned fund with low management expenses and low turnover, which can reduce taxes if you are investing in a personal taxable account.

If you work for an employer that has a company retirement plan such as a 401(k), this is a good place to start, as already discussed. You sign up with the benefits department and have money withheld from your pay and directed into a fund that you select. This money gets invested before you get a chance to spend it!

Or you can go directly to a mutual fund company to set

up an account and transfer money into the fund you choose—you can invest when you have extra money or commit to a regular investment schedule. It's up to you! The account you set up at the fund company can be a personal account or an IRA. The personal account is a taxable account—so if dividends are paid, they are taxable to you, or if you sell for a gain, that is taxed to you as well. That's not necessarily bad, but it is different from the IRA.

If you set up the account as an IRA, the money should be left invested until you are age fifty-nine and a half or older. If you take an early distribution, there is a tax penalty of 10 percent in addition to regular income taxes. However, if you leave this money to accumulate for decades, the dividends and any gains in the account are not taxed for years. This allows your money and all the gains to compound until you take money out of this account during retirement.

WORRY LESS, INVEST MORE

Once you have cash built up and lifestyle costs that are lower than your take-home pay, find a long-term investment. Start by looking at an established fund company. There are many reputable large companies.

Identify a low-cost, no-load fund. By low cost, I mean less than .10 percent or .20 percent in internal management costs at the most. No-load means there are no built-in sales charges or commissions to salespeople. This fund should be diversified with hundreds, maybe thousands, of stocks. Start with an amount you can leave invested for many years.

There was a time when people owned mostly individual stocks, and so they worried about the ups and downs of their accounts based on the performances of those stocks. It's possible for a company to go out of business, file for bankruptcy, or be low-priced for years. That's the risk in owning individual stocks. But owners of broadly diversified mutual funds don't have this worry of total loss. Sure, values will go down with the market—sometimes a lot! Declines of 20 percent to 30 percent or more are not uncommon. During the most severe times, values can even cut in half!

But familiarizing yourself with the history of the market will help you stay chill when markets decline. Don't try to guess the direction of the market in the short term but instead have confidence in long-term gains. Looking at historical evidence, a review of twenty-year rolling histories shows that annual average returns over this time period are much more predictable than over the course of five or ten years.

Longer terms, like thirty or forty years—which a twentysomething investor should be thinking about—have even more predictable results. Understanding and committing to a long-term view before making your first investment is the first step to successful investing in stocks or stock mutual funds.

In future years you may want to consider other investments such as real estate or business opportunities. But starting out, stock mutual fund investing makes sense because it requires smaller initial investments, is readily available to buy or sell, and requires little time and effort to maintain.

Money Mantra: I can change the trajectory of my money situation today, since I now know the how-tos of becoming a millionaire!

CHOOSE YOUR FINANCIAL FUTURE:

If you're excited to learn even more about catching the wave of long-term investing, read Chapter 12: Getting the Wind at Your Back. If you prefer to be

financially stagnant, go to the back of the book for
Financial Plan B.

Chapter 12

Getting the Wind at Your Back

HOW THE BOOKKEEPER'S DAUGHTER DID IT

There's nothing better than the feeling of having the wind at your back. Imagine how a tailwind makes brisk walking, running, or biking easier! It's far better than facing stiff headwinds. In your financial life, the same is true. Getting the financial wind at your back as soon as possible makes life, relationships, and your career all feel like a breeze.

Most people have two wealth-building engines:

1. The first engine is the work they do and the earnings they generate. If they can keep their expenses

less than their earnings, they build savings and financial capital. This is where most of us must start.

2. The second engine—and one that's potentially more powerful—is when the earnings on your accumulated assets and financial capital (investments) are greater than the interest cost on the capital you're borrowing (your home mortgage, student loans, and other debts).

You want to get to the point where both engines are firing on all cylinders. You're saving money from earnings, but you're also earning more from your accumulated money—your financial accounts and investments—than the cost of money you have borrowed. This is when your net worth grows at a rapid rate. Typically, this doesn't have an immediately noticeable impact on someone in their twenties or thirties, but it can with the right plan of action. With consistent effort, the effects compound and yield significant results that can accelerate throughout a lifetime.

The relationship between your earnings and the amount you save is almost entirely dependent on how you establish your lifestyle. If it's expensive—equal to or greater than your net earnings—well, the result is no savings. Many Americans, like the Surgeon, go through life this way. However, if you accumulate savings and investments with positive returns, and pay off or reduce loans and debts, cutting interest costs, your capital works for you!

Getting the financial wind at your back is important to plan for at every stage of your financial life. Set yourself up to have higher earnings from work, eliminate unnecessary expenses, and build savings and investments. Be wise in how you build your investment portfolio, add to your accounts, and pay down your debts. Get both of your financial engines working for you—your human capital (working and earning) and your financial capital (investments and savings). *When you are consistently adding to your investments because your income is greater than your expenses, and the long-term return on your investments is greater than the interest cost of your loans, this is when the financial wind is at your back!*

Once you begin the first phase, saving money and rightsizing your lifestyle to be less expensive than your income, it's time to decide how to handle your savings. If you do not have a cash reserve, a savings or money market account should be the first place you consider funding. After building some emergency reserve, you can begin long-term investing by starting or increasing your payroll deduction at work and funding the retirement savings plan your employer offers.

Many serious-for-the-first-time wealth builders have no cash reserve and no retirement savings but loads of debt to pay off. It's been my experience that many first-time investors can benefit from addressing all three—reserves, retirement, and debt—at once, but in smaller, reasonable amounts.

As an example, the first-timer might be best off by sending 3 percent to 4 percent of earnings to pay down credit card debt in addition to the minimum payment. Three percent could go to a cash reserve savings account toward a target balance. And you could opt for 3 percent to the company retirement savings plan, capturing an additional 3 percent from employer-matching payments. I typically advise paying more than the amount of an employer's match, but you've got to do what you've got to do when in a pinch.

THE BOOKKEEPER'S DAUGHTER

The Bookkeeper's daughter wasn't much interested in

financial matters. She graduated from college, finished a graduate degree program, and became a teacher. She traveled during the summers, loved meeting friends for "foodie" dinners, and was involved in charities and causes. She dressed well but didn't have expensive designer labels like some of her friends wore.

She had purchased a reliable hand-me-down car during college since she didn't want any car payments. She rented a nice home near the school where she taught, and it was tastefully decorated. When she purchased furniture and décor, she carefully contemplated and bought only good quality items she could keep for years without replacing. Her lifestyle was much like her family's—she lived comfortably but only spent what she could afford at that time. That means she didn't borrow money.

She worked part-time at an extra job and used this money to make additional principal payments on her college loan. Every month she had money left over and saved an increasing amount over the years. The money in her retirement plan was invested in a stock index mutual fund for the long run. She looked at the statements when they came in the mail, but she spent little time following the prices and the markets.

During the summer months when she had free time, she called me or stopped by my office for a review. Each year the results showed improvement. By her thirties she was saving money and making investment returns that equaled more than her savings. Her financial wind was picking up steam.

She's vaguely aware that her mom and dad are well off financially. But I doubt she thinks at all about a future inheritance, preferring to enjoy her own financial independence. She lives a life doing what she wants, within reason, and has few financial worries or concerns.

> **Money Mantra:** I can be comfortable now with the money I have and live large later, because being patient comes with an enormous payoff.

CHOOSE YOUR FINANCIAL FUTURE:

There may be a time when you want the assistance of a wealth advisor. Move on to Chapter 13: The Sea Captain and the Golf professional.

The Sea Captain and the Golf Professional

YOU'LL PROBABLY NEED ADVICE SOMEDAY—HERE'S WHERE TO GET IT

Bob retired as the captain of an ocean-going ship and returned to the Midwest to manage the family ranch in the Sandhills of Nebraska. He had little interest in financial matters, leaving those details to his wife, a retired advertising executive.

Once, as she and I were reviewing their financial plan, Bob walked into the kitchen and, in his captain's growl, said, *"Jeff, what the hell is it you actually do for us?"* Cautiously, I explained the role of a wealth advisor—to develop a custom plan and portfolio, to review financial results, and to compare them to future goals and objectives. An advisor should recommend alterations in the portfolio and actions to help people get back on track. I continued to explain the need for regular reviews to make sure investors never get too far off the path toward their goals.

He said, "What you do is a helluva lot like a ship captain's job, right?" I didn't know what to say. He continued, "When we left port, I'd set a course from 'Frisco to Hawaii, and then go about other duties for the day. Then later I would check our position, and see how the currents and the winds had pushed us off course, then I'd make corrections to get us back on a straight line to Honolulu. That's what you do for us."

I've shared this story with many of my real-life clients for the last couple of decades because it is true. My work is much like the role of a ship's captain. My clients pay an advisory fee for my advice and attention. In addition to building and monitoring investment portfolios, I offer guidance on financial issues such as funding college educations for children, retirement planning, and estate and wealth transfer decisions. Some people need someone like me to be the captain to steer their financial ship. This is probably not you right now, but it could be. Other people just need a little advice or a financial tune-up from time to time.

GOLF LESSONS

I'm not much of a golfer, but, ironically, I enjoy watching the sport on Sunday afternoons. Maybe my understanding of how difficult the game is inspires me to enjoy a relaxing afternoon watching the professionals.

Golf, however, comes easily for some people, some of the time. They hit the ball crisply, in such a relaxed way, and right on target. Putts roll straight to the hole, as if the ball had eyes. Other times, the same players hit poor shots that miss the fairway or the green or even find a sand trap or water hazard. Some days, even pro golfers can't make even the easiest of putts.

I've realized that, like investing, golf can be a real head game. This is when a player's scores can rise or fall based on their poise and focus on the game. Golf pros tell students not to get rattled by the last shot or the poor score on the previous hole. Forget about it, they say, and concentrate on the task at hand, the present shot.

Investors make similar mistakes. They invest while looking in the rearview mirror of life rather than out the windshield at the road ahead. They consider only the recent past and recent headlines, without developing and staying within a well-thought-out, repeatable strategy.

Because golf is not natural to me, every so often I get a tune-up from Mike, my favorite teaching professional. He keeps me focused on the important parts of the game. I always play the game consistently better and enjoy it more when I go back to the basics or have coaching sessions. I set up an appointment for a lesson only when I need it.

To support your investment and planning results, you might need to do the same. Maybe you don't need to pay for ongoing "sea captain" guidance. You may only need a boost in getting started or a tune-up like I get on my golf game. If you feel the need for ongoing comprehensive guidance you might decide to work with a financial professional on a regular basis. If you are more interested in financial assistance just to get started or as needed, you might work with a financial planner on a one-time engagement.

THE FIDUCIARY ADVISOR

With a little help, you can probably get started with the basics—building a cash reserve, paying down debts, and signing up to make contributions to an employer-provided retirement plan. If complications and questions surface, I recommend locating a fee-only advisor who is a fiduciary.

As a fiduciary, your advisor must give you advice that is in your best interest. Fee-only means the advisor doesn't get paid commissions or have hidden incentives to sell you anything. The advisor gets paid an agreed-upon amount, often an affordable hourly rate, for only the advice the investor needs.

How do you find such an advisor?

Whether you are looking for periodic advice or an ongoing advisory relationship, I recommend advisors who are affiliated with the National Association of Personal Financial Advisors (NAPFA). When the time comes for a review or an adjustment of your financial course, consider finding a NAPFA advisor who suits your needs.

NAPFA advisors are required to sign a pledge to act as

fiduciaries. They work *only* for a fee or engagement-based arrangement, never getting paid commissions or incentives to sell anything. They are required to maintain high standards in their practice as well as significant professional continuing education every two-year period.

You can locate an advisor or an advisory firm near you at the NAPFA.org website. Or, you can ask other trusted advisors, such as a CPA or an attorney, for the names of advisors they recommend. NAPFA advisors will likely be registered investment advisors (RIAs) as opposed to stockbrokers or investment salespeople. RIA firms are required to disclose any disputes or complaints with the Securities and Exchange Commission (SEC) on Form ADV. Before hiring an advisor, get a copy of this form, and ask the advisor about any questions that arise from this report.

RIAs are compensated by the fees you, the client, pay. A fiduciary advisor is responsible to give you the advice that is right for you. Most stockbrokers and investment salespeople get paid commissions for selling you an investment, which can lead to conflicts of interest, and they may not have the requirement to act as a fiduciary when advising you.

My firm, Buckingham Strategic Wealth, is a registered investment advisor and a member of NAPFA.

Some people are naturally good with financial matters, doing a very fine job managing their finances by themselves. But not that many people are truly savvy at giving and taking their own financial advice, from what I've seen. Sometimes the cost of paying for advice is far less than the cost of making mistakes or delaying actions. That does not mean all financial professionals will give you the advice and recommendations you need, so proceed with caution.

Take as much time identifying and screening your professional advisor as you would in examining investments or other important decisions. To end this chapter, I've included a wealth advisor questionnaire for you to use in interviewing prospective financial professionals who might advise you. Good luck as you grab the opportunity to build a bigger, better life.

QUESTIONS TO ASK A FINANCIAL ADVISOR CANDIDATE

1. **How and why did you get into the wealth management and financial planning business?** If

they respond by talking about their interest in the market or focus on investment products only—or, worse, can't really answer the question—you might want to move on. Stockbroker types who like to play with other people's money are rarely valuable advisors. A pretty good response might be, "I was always good with money, and I really enjoy helping people."

2. **Where and how did you learn the business of being a financial planner?** "I had sales training with my company" is not a good answer. Experience is the best teacher in most professions, and that is certainly true with financial management. It's preferable if your prospective advisor has received solid experience and mentoring over classroom or company training.

3. **What is your process? How would we work together?** Look for a definite process and a clear, understandable explanation. Whatever it is, be sure your prospective advisor or financial firm has a proven, successful, and repeatable approach that can be put to work for you.

4. **What is your investment methodology?** You want to hear about something that is specific, tested, and repeatable. The investments recommended should also be tailored to your unique circumstances and

preferences. If they say, "I follow my firm's model portfolio," or something trite like, "I buy low, sell high," you might want to keep looking.

5. **How often would you meet or communicate with me if I were your client?** Write down the advisor's responses because sometimes even well-meaning financial professionals don't make good on their promises once they have your money under management and are earning fees. You should feel that contact is adequate and that it would involve two-way communication.

6. **Who will be doing the work? Do you work alone or have a team that will serve me?** If a team is involved, ask to meet the other members and learn about their specialties or value to you if you become a client. Try to learn and under-stand the depth of their experience if they will be involved. If the wealth planner works alone, who will give you advice when they are in a meeting, away from the office, or on vacation?

7. **How much will I be involved as your client?** If you want to be part of the process, and I highly suggest that you should be, make sure the financial advisor intends to keep you involved and can tell you their plans for your ongoing exchange of ideas.

8. **What are your fees and what, if any, conflicts**

do you have in serving me? The main thing you are looking for here is full disclosure. Consider the total package—what's offered in the way of services versus the cost of the advice. Make notes so you remember what was said.

9. **If I become a client and then become dissatisfied, how can I exit our relationship?** This is a very important question, if for no other reason than it immediately translates as, "I will not settle for lackluster work. If you don't follow through on your promises, I will find someone who will."

10. **Can you explain to me the first steps we would take if I decide to become a client?** Well-organized and experienced financial professionals should have a predefined new client experience they can explain.

Money Mantra: I've learned I can get started saving and investing on my own, but when I need professional guidance I now know how to find it.

CHOOSE YOUR FINANCIAL FUTURE:

Looking for a final pep talk to get your financial headspace straight? Turn the page for the Conclusion. Feel free to skip Plan B altogether.

Conclusion

In this book you've learned more than the basics on how to accumulate money and multiply your wealth, but most of all, the importance of starting your savings in your twenties. Your first step is to adjust your lifestyle expenses, reducing some unnecessary costs. I've observed that some of the greatest deterrents to getting started in accumulating money are expensive cars, overspending on a home, entertainment costs, and lifestyle expenses that don't necessarily have to be eliminated but just need to be controlled.

You've learned the importance of saving every time you handle money. And whether it's a small amount or a large amount, you know it's critical that you set aside some money every time you touch it. You need to set up a cash reserve savings account so you'll have some amount of money that's available for emergencies and for planned or unplanned purchases, such as a new refrigerator when your old one is not working.

And now you know it's important to build a long-term savings program that includes retirement accounts and investments with a lifelong view. Owning the right-sized, right-priced home is also critical. Renting until you get a financial base might be a better idea than buying a home for now.

Avoiding high-cost debt to purchase consumer items or cover unnecessary expenses isn't easy when you are starting out as a financially independent adult, but it is critical. Having zero credit card balances and installment payments gives you an opportunity to save, invest, and accumulate money.

WHY YOU SHOULD DO ALL OF THE ABOVE

First off, buying lots of stuff and excess material goods really doesn't make you happy. There might be a thrill when you buy something new, but it wears off quickly. Then you might be left with a credit card bill or loan to pay off.

I've observed the great value of having healthy financial habits in place. Immediately obvious is the low stress of people who are financially secure and how financial freedom affects them and the people they love. People who are in financial control experience a certain feeling of confidence. This confidence usually enhances a successful marriage and an enjoyable family life. It means raising children in a healthy way and providing for education at various levels.

It means sometimes being able to consider career and work opportunities that might otherwise not be possible, such as having the ability to start a small business rather than working for a low hourly rate. It might even mean that early in life, work will be optional altogether! Having excess cash or assets also opens opportunities to support your important charities, causes, and religious organizations.

The only tradeoff for all of these benefits is perhaps cutting back spending early in life to instead save money and begin growing wealth in your twenties! It's a pretty good tradeoff.

Here's a checklist of how you can put this plan into action:

- ☐ Evaluate your everyday spending and adjust as necessary. Do this periodically. What gets measured, gets managed.
- ☐ Avoid overspending on larger purchases, such as home, cars, leisure, and entertainment.
- ☐ Open a savings reserve account and make deposits every time you get money.
- ☐ Pay cash whenever possible rather than borrowing money or using credit.
- ☐ When you take out a loan, apply smart borrowing with good debt only.
- ☐ Contribute to a 401(k) and IRA, for your retirement-age investment money only.
- ☐ Track and monitor your progress regularly with a NAPFA advisor or other professional.

Financial Plan B

I sometimes recommend Plan B when I talk with clients who are at the end of their working career, if they are short the amount of money it would take to live their ideal life during retirement. Usually, they are initially disappointed and a little sad when I explain this to them.

That's because Plan B means a reduction in lifestyle. Clients often have to move into lower-cost housing, downsizing to a smaller home or even moving to an apartment. They often need to opt for inexpensive used cars, possibly selling a car and owning only one car. They sometimes change travel plans and eliminate some pastimes, club memberships, and even charitable contributions.

For most of these people I've worked with, after the

initial shock wears off, scaling down is not that big of a burden. But sometimes there is a significant adjustment in their self-esteem and even embarrassment.

However, if you are reading this last section of my book, it's likely you're a young person who's embarking on a career. You're just entering your adult life. Based on my contact with my former college students, I've discovered that some intentionally choose a Plan B lifestyle.

Let me introduce you to a young woman I'll call Sally. She spent very little time in college, quickly leaving higher education and taking a job she enjoys in the service industry. She deliberately lives modestly, setting her attitude and objectives accordingly. She saves money but not very much because she doesn't need very much. When I asked her why she seems to lack ambition, she glared and snapped, "I am ambitious about doing what I want!"

Well, who can argue with that?

But the argument is this: maybe her life goals and situation will change in a few years, and she will wish she had some money accumulated and fewer debts rather than only the memories of fun times in her twenties.

Implementing a Plan B lifestyle early in life is very similar to implementing a Plan B lifestyle at the end of a working career. If you're a young reader, a twenty-something adult, and you either blatantly reject the practice of saving money early or you just don't do it, a Plan B lifestyle can and should be implemented right now.

Here's what it looks like: Sally decided she didn't really need to own a home and that she would rent until there was a strong reason she really needed to buy a house. She valued her independence from financial matters and relationships so that she was able to make changes in where she rented her home or apartment. Sally bought a reliable used car that was several years old, and she was actually pretty good at taking care of it and kept it for a long time.

A coupon clipper and value shopper, Sally ate most meals at home except when she spotted favorite happy hour specials. She bought some of her clothes at a thrift shop or consignment stores. She earned enough money from bartending and serving a few nights per week to cover her living costs.

I'm sure there's more to her story that has unfolded

or will develop over the years. The impressive point is that she has chosen to live a lower-cost lifestyle… for a lifetime. Sally did not have debt, which is the heavy black cloud that hangs over those who sometimes go for years before facing the dire situation. But Sally didn't have much savings or any long-term investments either.

Like Sally and the Surgeon's son, many people have opted for a Plan B lifestyle—they just don't know it yet! They save minimally or not at all, and they handle finances much like Sally does but expect something completely different at the end of a working career. Possibly they hope for some financial miracle or a large inheritance.

Creating and implementing a Plan B lifestyle isn't really that hard. It is, however, sometimes hard for some to accept. The point of this section is to make sure you realize it should be a measured choice to live this way and not come as a surprise.

To live young, wild, and free is to prioritize spending for fun—whatever that means to you—as more important than establishing a larger, financially secure life for you and your future family. It means you have enough to get by, but sometimes you might have to accept the financial pressures that accompany lack of money. That's okay, as long as you are ready for it and it won't impact your comfort and enjoyment.

My maternal grandfather lived a Plan B life. He never owned his home but always rented. And he never trusted banks or investment companies. He worked for the local telephone company for thirty-seven years, but he never saved or invested any money—oh, if he had only purchased some shares of the company he worked for!

But he refused to carry any debt, spending everything he earned but *only* what he earned. On payday, he cashed his check, paid his bills, and put the leftover money in an envelope and made it last until the next payday. He did benefit from a company pension and Social Security benefits, and he lived simply but comfortably well into his eighties.

He was a wonderful grandpa to me and my brother and sister! When he passed, he had no debts but left a small cash amount to my mom and her sister. He had a few favorite items, especially a Browning shotgun he left to me. I've never fired it.

My financial advice for a young person interested in a Plan B lifestyle is to find an employer that offers a defined benefit pension. A few companies, the military, and some government agencies have these pension plans that pay an income for life at retirement. These companies usually pay lower salaries, but the pension minimizes or eliminates the need to save money for retirement—especially if you are okay spending only what you earn, like my grandpa.

Recommended Reading

UNDERSTANDING COMPOUNDING

The Slight Edge (Turning Simple Disciplines into Massive Success and Happiness), Jeff Olson

PLANNING YOUR FUTURE

Think and Grow Rich, Napoleon Hill

The One Thing, Gary Keller with Jay Papasan

The Road Less Stupid, Keith Cunningham

The Millionaire Next Door, Dr. Thomas Stanley

RETIREMENT PLANNING ADVICE

Fund Your Future: A Tax Smart Savings Plan In Your 20s and 30s (2020 Edition), Ed Slott, CPA

INVESTING

Think, Act, and Invest Like Warren Buffett, Larry E. Swedroe

Any of the books by the late John C. Bogle

IT'S NOT ALL ABOUT THE MONEY

The Monk Who Sold His Ferrari, Robin Sharma

Acknowledgments

I rely on input from multiple sources. Thank you to my important editors and contributors:

Cris Trautner and Aaron Vacin of Infusionmedia, my editors and advisors on everything I've ever written.

Gerry Finnegan, CFP®, a respected colleague in the financial industry and later a fellow instructor at the University of Nebraska-Lincoln.

Dan Vodvarka, a one-time sportswriter and editor, and my friend for fifty years.

The incredibly talented Nick Ledden of Buckingham Strategic Wealth, Tucker Max, and everyone at Scribe Media.